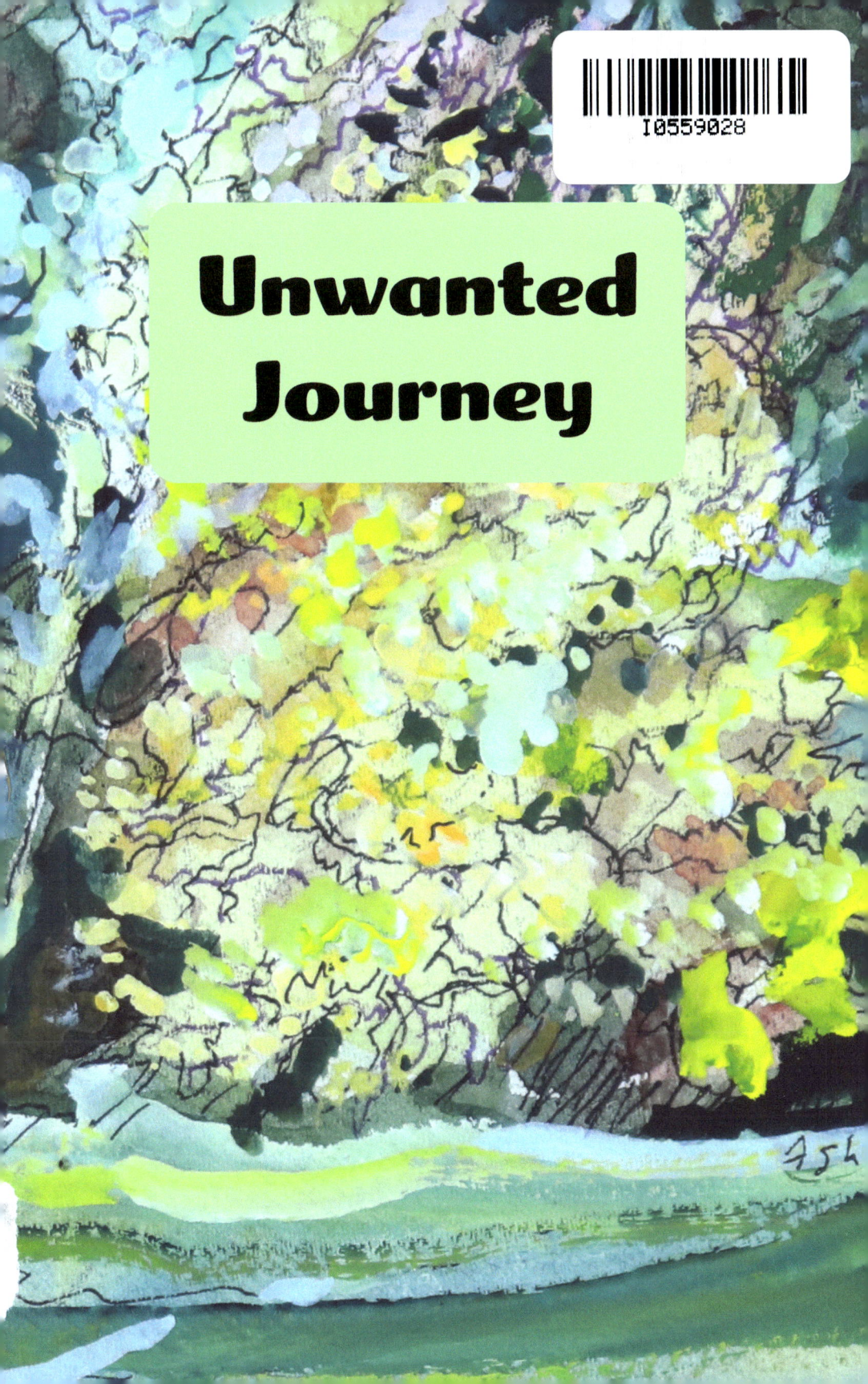

Unwanted Journey

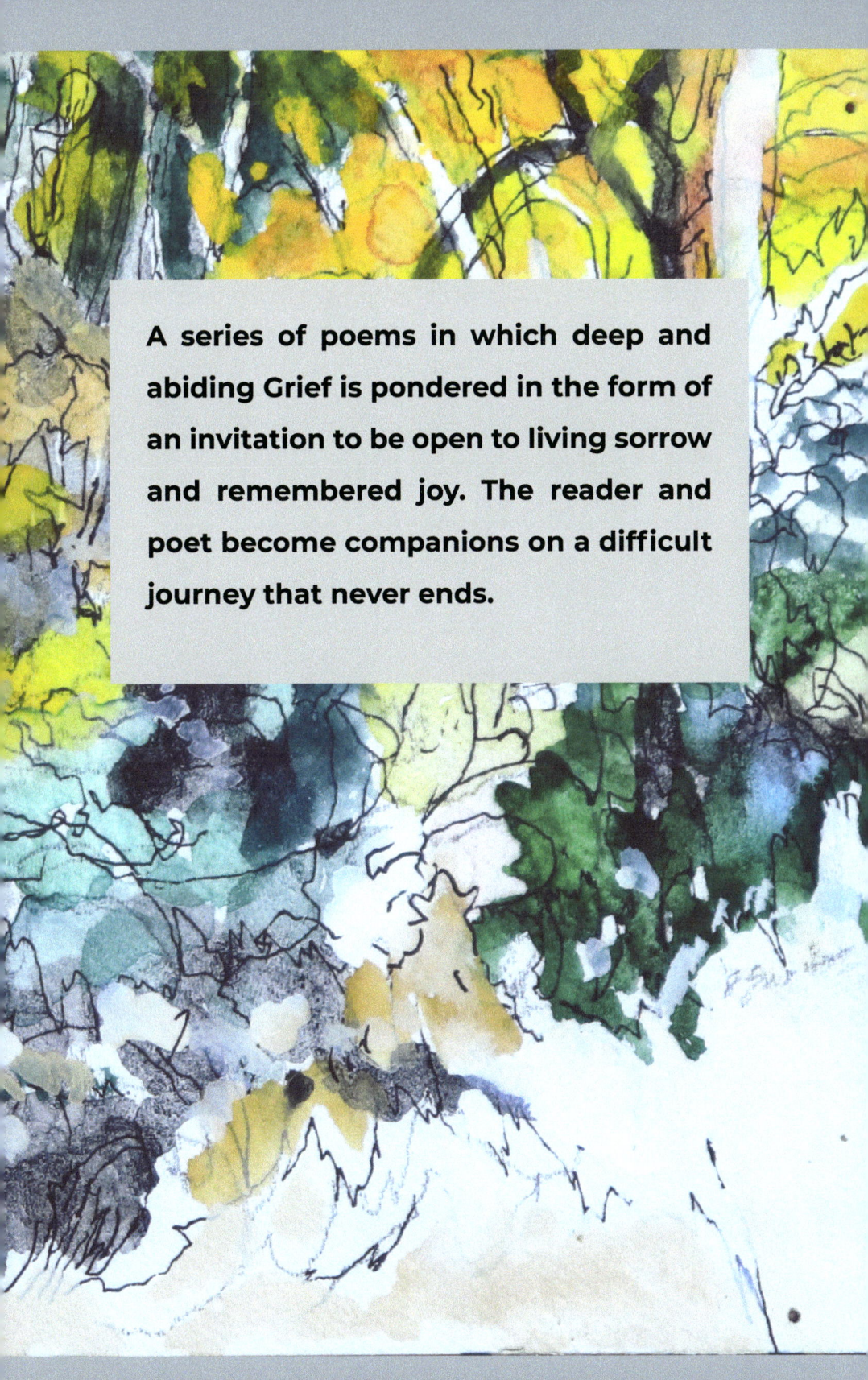

A series of poems in which deep and abiding Grief is pondered in the form of an invitation to be open to living sorrow and remembered joy. The reader and poet become companions on a difficult journey that never ends.

ISBN: 978-1-958150-23-8
Unwanted Journey

First printing August 2025

Published by **Inner Peace Press**
Eau Claire, Wisconsin, USA
www.innerpeacepress.com

to Steve

If

If I could gather the words,
harness them, arrange them on
paper with my pen,
I would.

This wisdom found in grief,
A gentle understanding of wasted
moments and fully lived days
too often taken for granted.
The uneasy shift of time and space.

Beloved poetry has new meaning.

If
I could walk with you,
in the quiet of a forest
perhaps my words would move
with the wind through the
leaves
to clarify, simplify.

Words searching
for a home in metaphoric rhetoric.
    I would whisper them, or
write them in prose,
or share them in quiet moments,
if I could.

Seeking Strength

Grief, love's opposite;

An unwanted journey into self;

Rediscovering the tenets of faith,

Seeking courage

however, finding

new meaning in the words of

scripture, poetry, song, and

  the words are inadequate.

Too weary to begin

yet I move forward, moving

Into the daylight to stand among

Shadows and movement;

the veil between

Peripheral vision; Presence

Sheer, Unknown,

Shadows and movement bring comfort

accompaniment forward.

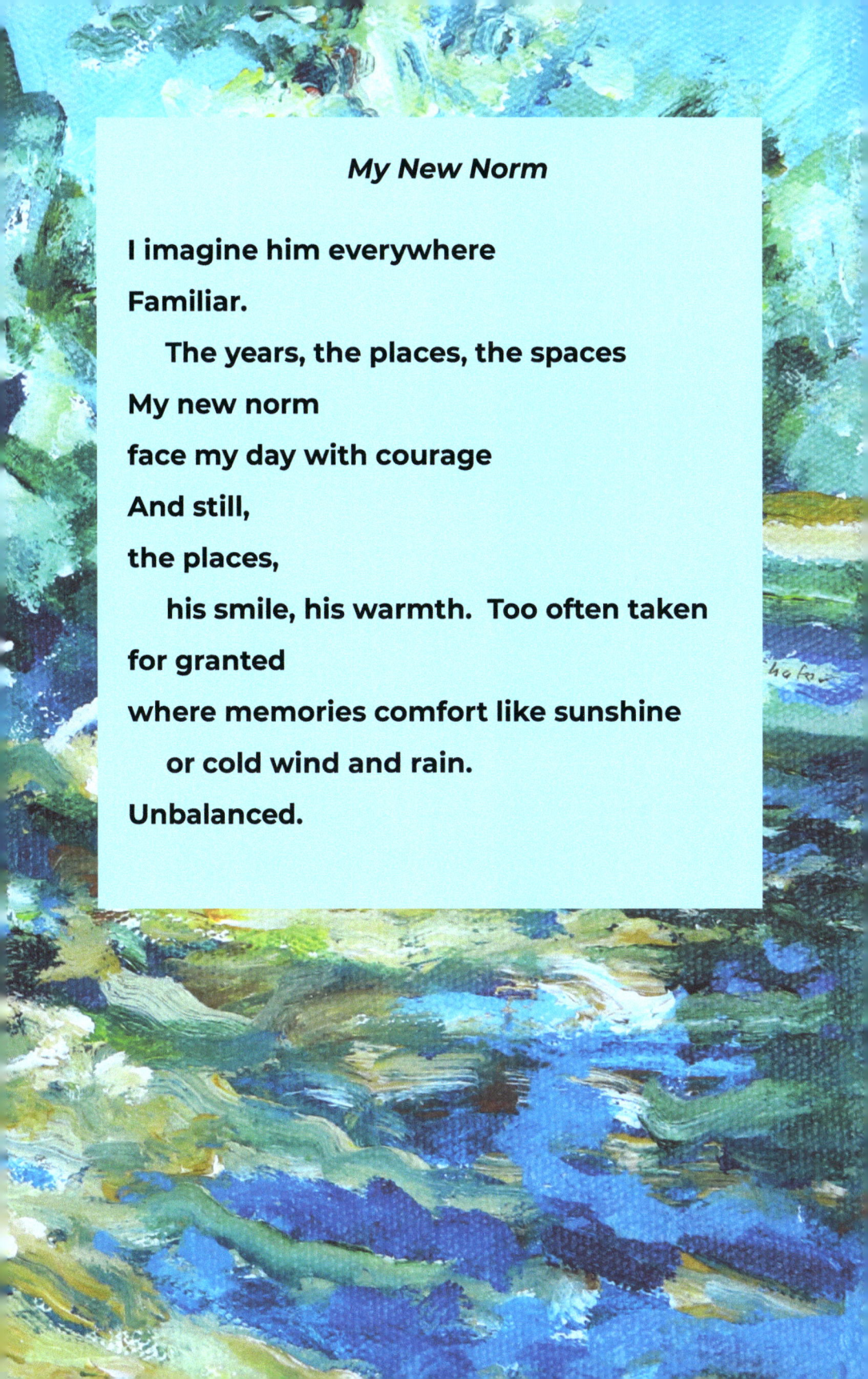

My New Norm

I imagine him everywhere
Familiar.
    The years, the places, the spaces
My new norm
face my day with courage
And still,
the places,
    his smile, his warmth. Too often taken
for granted
where memories comfort like sunshine
    or cold wind and rain.
Unbalanced.

Longing

Longing
to touch his face
and feel his skin
to trace his smile
to look into his eyes
to remember unconditional love
to believe and hope
and laugh from the core of my being
to experience the solace in the
warmth of his embrace
to feel his touch
       his touch.

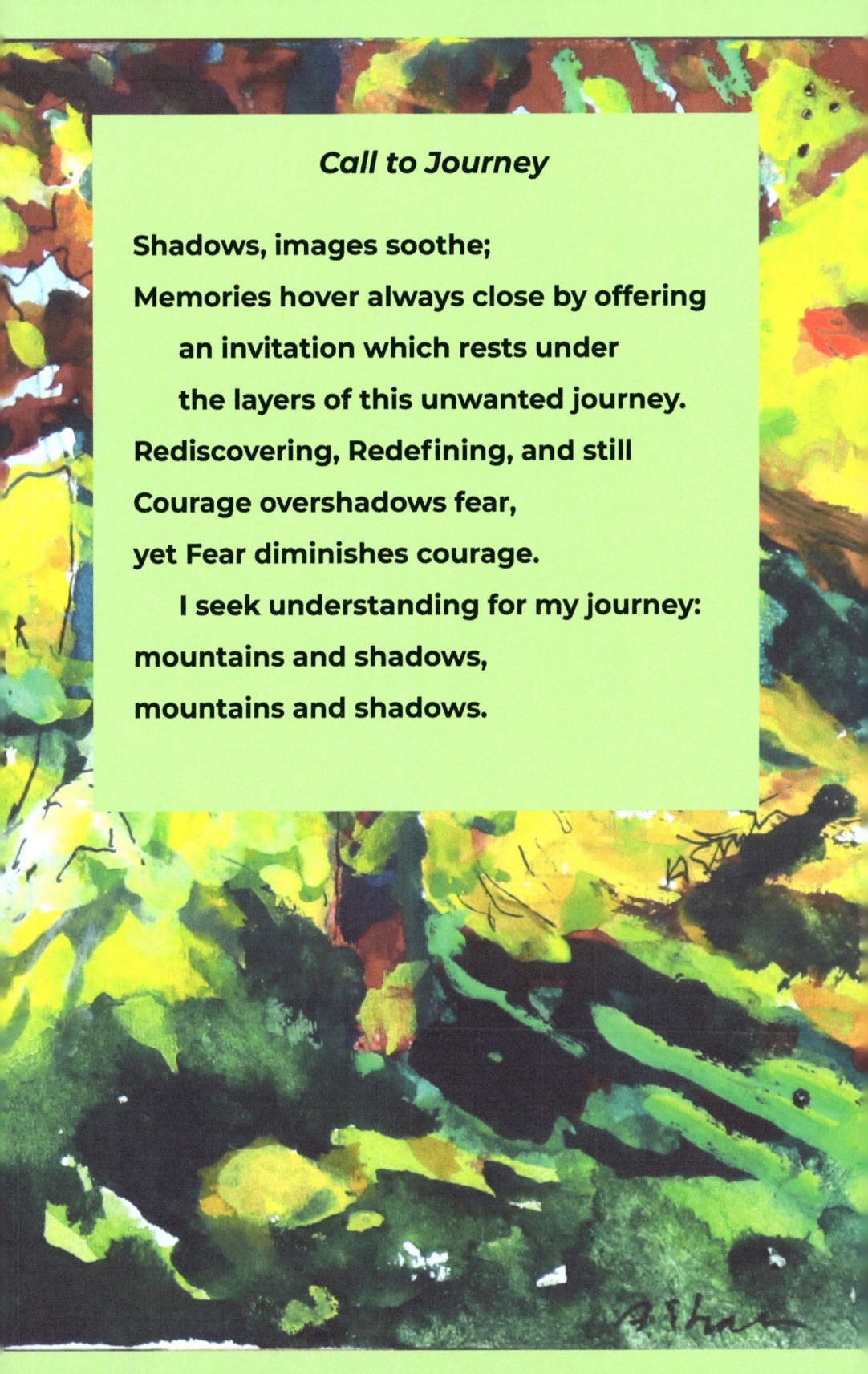

Call to Journey

Shadows, images soothe;

Memories hover always close by offering

    an invitation which rests under

    the layers of this unwanted journey.

Rediscovering, Redefining, and still

Courage overshadows fear,

yet Fear diminishes courage.

    I seek understanding for my journey:

mountains and shadows,

mountains and shadows.

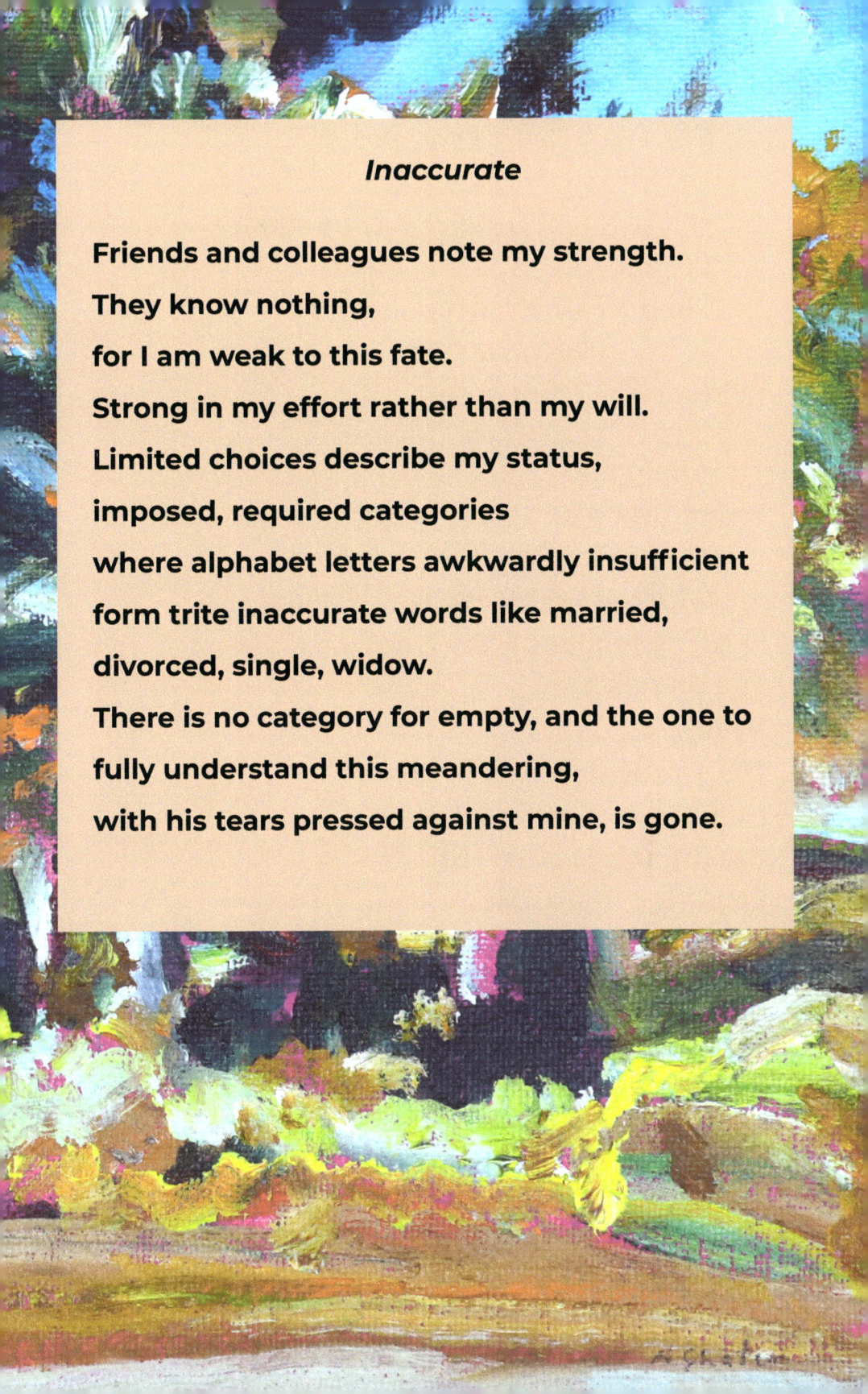

Inaccurate

Friends and colleagues note my strength.
They know nothing,
for I am weak to this fate.
Strong in my effort rather than my will.
Limited choices describe my status,
imposed, required categories
where alphabet letters awkwardly insufficient
form trite inaccurate words like married,
divorced, single, widow.
There is no category for empty, and the one to
fully understand this meandering,
with his tears pressed against mine, is gone.

Learning

When did it feel strange having dinner
with friends.
Uneven placement of chairs,
　　　　　like an echo:
he's gone . . . he's gone . . .

Then came
awareness that dinner invitations disappeared
　and a realization that
　I, with my misplaced social skills,
　am no longer on the couple-list.
I do understand.
Really.
Our world goes two-by-two.
I set out on a new journey.
Except, this is different.
Each step unwanted.
Arduous.
　You who accompanied me,
　I have never asked you why
　You see me as I am today.　　Thank you.

I have learned from you.

Those Eyes

Neither ice packs

Nor expensive creams

Can erase what

Grief owns.

Sunglasses hide, eyedrops soothe

And then, staring into a looking glass

The wholeness of loss stares back.

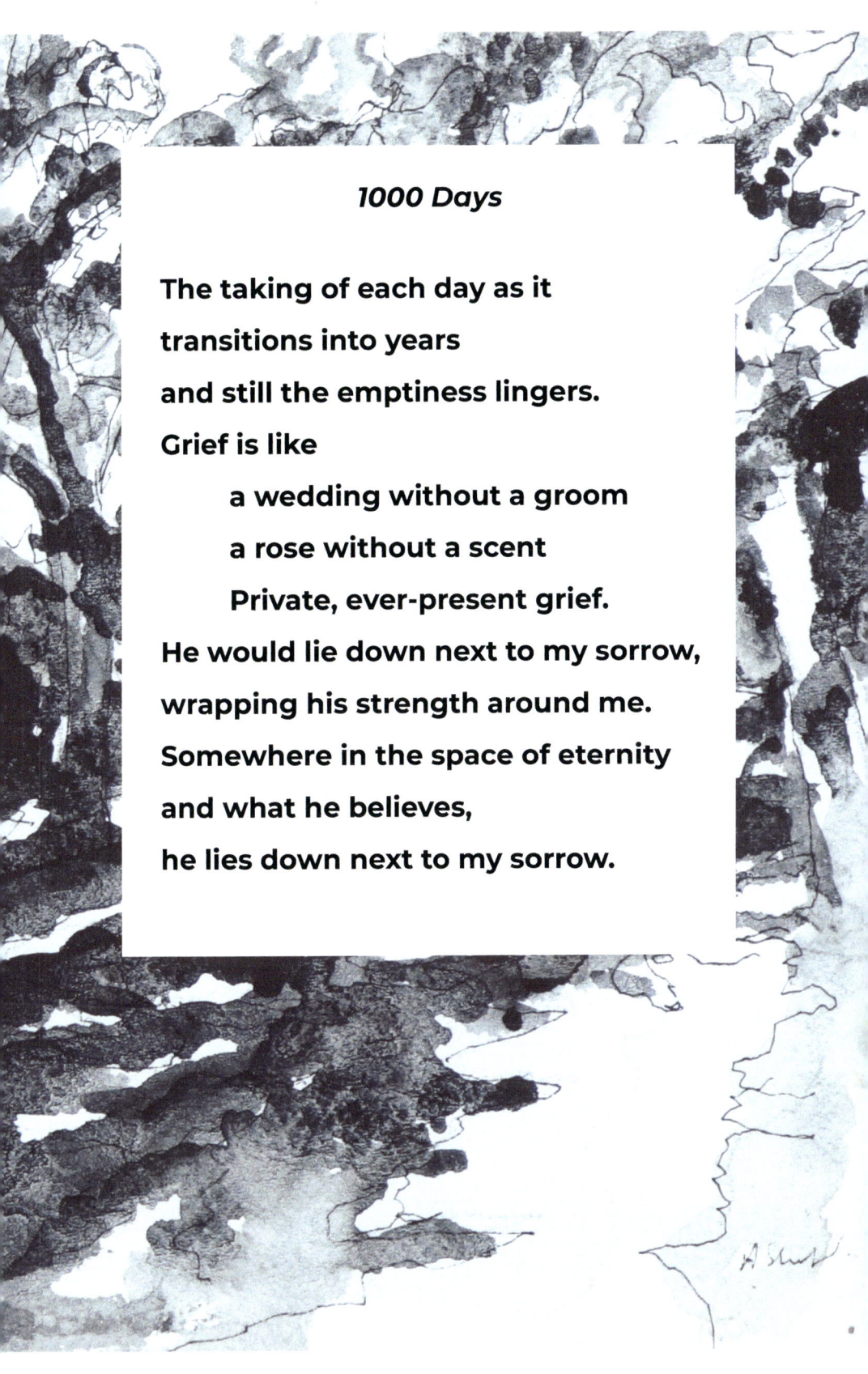

1000 Days

The taking of each day as it
transitions into years
and still the emptiness lingers.
Grief is like

    a wedding without a groom

    a rose without a scent

    Private, ever-present grief.

He would lie down next to my sorrow,
wrapping his strength around me.
Somewhere in the space of eternity
and what he believes,
he lies down next to my sorrow.

In Accordance

It is real, this melancholy understanding
that being alone
has become
in accordance with life. I no longer wait
for him
to turn the key
in the lock, to enter with his attitude of appreciation.
     In my world
     I arrive home and delve into activities
some planned,
others not.
I have
abundant time and
space,
scant any level of content.
When I walk up the street,
or near shops, I am
acquainted with the ritual of
unfamiliar faces passing by,
acceptance of the strangeness
of being alone,
that no one
has required me to inform my whereabouts,
nor have I thought to do so,
becoming familiar with the fact that no one
knows where I am.
Uneasy steps guide
each awareness,
and still
I seek the desire to be
me.

I Want My Life Back

I want my life back, the life before . . .
    The one where he reached for my hand
and we walked in silence.
Our decades together,
a life so often seasoned with surprises.

I want
that life;
our life.
Mindful thought, real and basic,
reminds me often
that my life ended with his.
    Oh, not the self that I am,
    the we that we were.
An earned place in time;
lessons learned and life celebrated.
I want that life,
where each morning brought his voice,
"good morning, love" to a room, now silent.

Cover

Introduction

If

Seeking Strength

My New Norm

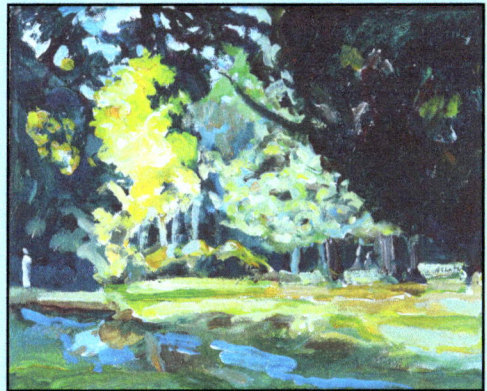

Longing

Call to Journey

Inaccurate

Learning

Those Eyes

1000 Days

In Accordance

I Want My Life Back

Judith Day

As a young woman I became interested in writing poetry. Rather than share my poems, I kept them in a treasured box at the top of my closet. Going back to college in midlife, I was drawn to a variety of writing courses, ending my college work with a BA is English at California State University and later a MA in World Literature. I found the love of learning and became a teacher for 20 years, winning four awards as Most Inspirational Teacher and, most importantly, the respect of my students and parents.

One November evening my life changed and I found myself learning about Grief with the sudden death of my beloved husband. After several intimate renderings, I found a measure of solace in writing. Without a plan, I could see the poems sharing lessons and love in a journey like no other.

Anders C. Shafer is an Emeritus Professor at the University of Wisconsin–Eau Claire, where he was the Max Schoenfeld Distinguished Professor. He taught painting, drawing, and illustration for 43 years.

A practicing professional artist, he has works in many museums including: The Smithsonian, the Allen Museum, Portland Museum of Art, and the Sheldon Museum. He has won over a hundred awards and been in countless exhibitions. His best known book is The Fantastic Journey of Pieter Bruegel, published by Dutton's Children's Books, New York.

www.ingramcontent.com/pod-product-compliance
Lightning Source LLC
Chambersburg PA
CBHW040853120626
46547CB00006B/591